Mort Künstler's

OLD WEST

COWBOYS

Mort Künstler's

OLD WEST

COWBOYS

Mort Künstler

RUTLEDGE HILL PRESS®

Nashville, Tennessee

Published by Rutledge Hill Press®, 211 Seventh Avenue North,
Nashville, Tennessee 37219. Distributed in Canada by H. B. Fenn & Company, Ltd.,
34 Nixon Road, Bolton, Ontario L7E 1W2. Distributed in Australia by The Five Mile
Press Pty., Ltd., 22 Summit Road, Noble Park, Victoria 3174. Distributed in
New Zealand by Tandem Press, 2 Rugby Road, Birkenhead, Auckland 10.
Distributed in the United Kingdom by Verulam Publishing, Ltd., 152a Park Street
Lane, Park Street, St. Albans, Hertfordshire AL2 2AU.

Jacket and text design by Bruce Gore/Gore Studio, Inc.
Color separations by NEC Incorporated

Library of Congress Cataloging-in-Publication Data

Künstler, Mort.
    [Old West]
    Mort Künstler's Old West: Cowboys / Mort Künstler
        p.   cm.
    A collection of Mort Künstler's Old West paintings depicting cowboy life on
the plains.
    ISBN 1-55853-588-8 (hb)
    1. Künstler, Mort—Catalogs. 2. Cowboys in art—Catalogs. 3. West
(U.S.)—In art—Catalogs.   I. Title.
ND237.K85A4   1998
759.13—dc21
                                                                    98-16102
                                                                    CIP

Printed in the United States of America
1 2 3 4 5 6 7 8 9 — 02 01 00 99 98

Contents

Introduction

As a kid growing up in Brooklyn during the Depression of the '30s and the wartime '40s, going to the movies every Saturday with my friends became a ritual. For ten cents we traveled into the past for a few hours to laugh, be thrilled, or cry. It was a great way to escape from the troubles of the world.

For laughs, there were the Marx Brothers, Laurel and Hardy, and the Three Stooges. For thrills, tears, laughter, and adventure all wrapped up in one, there were westerns. John Wayne, Gene Autry, Randolph Scott, and Roy Rogers were household names. Because of the popularity of the genre, every major star, including Jimmy Stewart, Henry Fonda, James Cagney, Humphrey Bogart, Clark Gable, and Frank Sinatra, eventually made westerns. Naturally, one of our most popular street games was cowboys and Indians.

I showed a talent for drawing at an early age, and my parents encouraged me in every way. After art training at Brooklyn College, UCLA, and Pratt Institute, I made my way into the bustling world of publishing in New York City. The assignments I sought most often were those with western themes. Soon I was doing paintings that appeared on the covers of some of the most popular books of all time. Western writers like Zane Grey, Max Brand, Louis L'Amour, and Dee

Brown had my covers on their books! I could not believe my good fortune—and to think I was actually paid for doing it! Eventually I painted a lot of advertising art for movies such as *Oklahoma Crude* with George C. Scott and *Breakheart Pass* with Charles Bronson.

In 1977 I staged my first one-man exhibition at the prestigious Hammer Galleries in New York City. My theme was the Old West. The show was a success and marked a significant change in my career. I gave up the financial security of illustration and commissioned work for the fun of painting whatever I wanted. People responded by buying the paintings. After a while, publishers approached me to buy the rights to reproduce these paintings for book covers. I was back on the book covers with one enormous difference: I was painting what I wanted without any interference from the publisher.

In this book, *Mort Künstler's Old West: Cowboys*, and its companion book, *Mort Künstler's Old West: Indians*, I have selected some paintings from the hundreds I have done over a period of more than forty-five years to bring some of the magic, excitement, glamour, and adventure of the West to others. Perhaps these paintings will help show the excitement which was felt about that bygone era and stimulate an interest to learn about that epic period in our history.

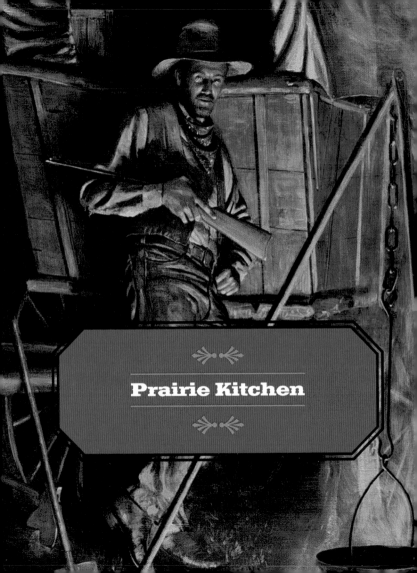

Prairie Kitchen

While I was working on a series of

paperback book covers in 1972, I painted close-ups of each of the heroes in different situations. To be sure that the reader did not confuse one book with another, I used different colors, which also gave a unique mood to each painting. This blue cover belongs to a series of novels written by Burt Arthur.

The character in this portrait is an important part of the history and myth of the Wild West. Called a "fast-draw artist" or a "gunman," he is a gunslinger who, in a western, starts or settles trouble.

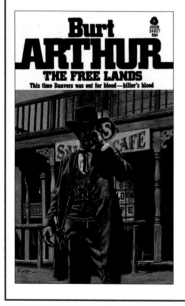

In real life, the gunslinger's belt and holster were called his "rig." His favored pistol was the Colt .45 "Peacemaker." Some adept gunslingers wore a two-gun rig, sometimes with the pistol butts facing forward, indicating they were good and fast at the "cross draw." Most gunslingers, however, never took part in what writers came to call "the walkdown," the dramatic scene in which the hero and villain stood at opposite ends of the street then walked slowly toward one another until someone drew his gun and someone hit the ground.

The Kansan

The title of this painting comes from the 1973 Zane Grey paperback published by Avon. The painting is based on a fabulous, stunted pine I saw near Cody, Wyoming. Immediately I knew that the tree and the nearby rock would make a great picture. The brown-and-yellow color scheme, with the sun down and the sky still light, add to the drama of the moment. Because I find pure landscape painting less interesting and not as challenging, I like to incorporate figures and horses into them. We do not know if this is a cowboy watching a herd of cattle, a lawman looking for an outlaw, or an outlaw being chased by a posse.

In history and in the movies, the two opposing sides were usually the established moneyed interests—cattle kings, lumber barons, land companies—and poor independent stockmen, farmers, and woodsmen. Often the big interests were successful because they held sway in water-rights disputes and in the use of open ranges. Defeats in open court or in the court of public opinion often made these men more determined to have their way, giving rise to the dubious profession of the hired gun.

Early Snow

Winters were always

dangerous for cattle and cowboys. Herds were usually moved into lower pastures in the fall. Occasionally, an early autumn snow caught everyone unprepared, and the cattlemen were compelled to move the herds out of the mountains before the snows deepened.

In the mountains and the northern plains, the livestock were kept close and cared for constantly. Range cattle could not find grass beneath the snow and had no instinct for eating snow when they could not find water.

Following the big "Die-Out" during the monstrously harsh winter of 1886–87 —when mountain ranchers lost 30 to 80 percent of their herds to mammoth blizzards—cattlemen changed their practices. They stored hay to feed the cattle in winter, culled weak animals from the herd for slaughter and skinning, and began breeding cattle with heavier coats and more insulating body fat.

In the painting the blue-gray tones and the falling snow help to set the mood and tell the story. The sheer beauty of the quiet snow contrasts the imminent danger and urgency the cattlemen feel.

Night Riders

In the violent, nearly lawless West, night riders were viewed with suspicion. Most honest, law-abiding men had no need to be away from home during the evening. Far too often, activity after dark meant that someone was up to no good. They might be cattle rustlers, horse thieves, robbers, or vigilantes.

Serious nighttime scrapes strained relations between the United States and Mexico, but Texans were losing tens of thousands of steers to rustlers from south of the border. Ranching giant Richard King lost $1 million in cattle, and in February and March 1875 twice fought off attacks on his ranch house by Mexican raiders. A power in the Lone Star State, King turned his home into a fort and encouraged the Texas Rangers' nighttime retaliation raids. The courage and persistence of the Texas night riders paid off. The Mexican gangs gave up their rustling ways by late 1876.

In 1875 Texas cattlemen had their own war with Mexican rustlers, resulting in countless scenes like this one. Cowboys and Texas Rangers would ride across the Mexican border at night, attack rustler camps, then ride north again, pursued by gangs or by the Mexican army.

In this painting, I tried to capture as much action as possible. I thought a chase scene would be exciting, and I achieved this by having some of the men look back while their horses are in full gallop. When I finished the painting, I felt I had succeeded in my goals, but I did not really know how well my work would be received by others until years later. Several paperback book publishers requested the rights to reproduce this painting on book covers. Segments were used, images were reversed, and eventually *Night Riders* was used on seven different book covers by five different publishers and six different authors. I am quite sure this is a record.

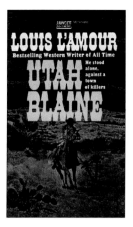

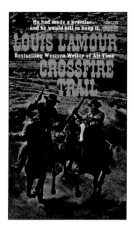

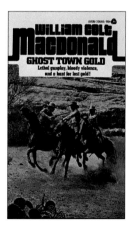

Call to Freedom

The idea for this painting, among

others, came from my friend, the late John Davidson of Vancouver.

The men who trapped wild horses and ponies for sale were called mustangers or mustang runners. One of their most effective methods of trapping these animals was to drive them into a concealed corral or into a box canyon (a dead-end or a no-outlet canyon) with a narrow entrance that was easy to block.

Completely undomesticated mustangs followed a dominant male stallion, who had fought other males to achieve leadership of the herd and to maintain most of its mares as his personal harem. His survival and fighting skills were superior, and the herd would follow his calls and lead. In this painting, the head stallion has escaped and

called to the herd, which breaks the fence and runs for freedom.

Studying the horses at the A-Bar-A Ranch in Encampment, Wyoming, helped me to do this painting, but I had difficulty with the lighting effect. With so many horses in the painting, I decided to make a sculpture to aid me. I then used a lamp and posed the clay horse in any position with the light exactly the way I wanted it. This technique was of immeasurable help in doing the painting.

When Richard Lynch, director of the Hammer Galleries, came to my studio to discuss an upcoming exhibition, he noticed the clay model I had sculpted and asked who did it. I said I had and explained why. He suggested I have it cast in bronze, and we placed a limited-edition of twenty in the show at the gallery in 1985. They quickly sold out. That horse remains the only sculpture I have ever created.

Charcoal preliminary sketch

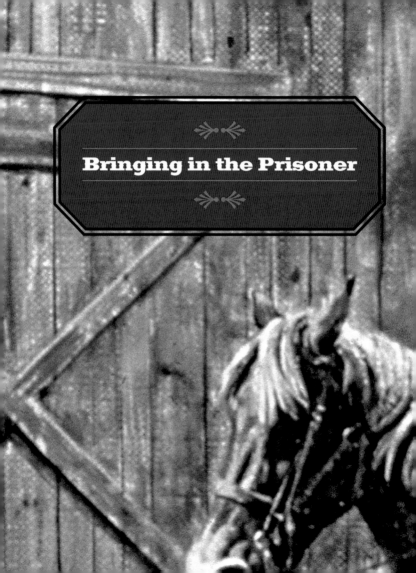

Bringing in the Prisoner

John Davidson called me shortly after my October 1979 show at Hammer Galleries with the idea for this painting. He even suggested that the prisoner should grasp his shoulder to help tell the story. I thought it would make a great picture. Most of the time I cannot use the subjects people suggest for my paintings, but John unfailingly came up with great ideas. Ten of my paintings—some of my best western works—were John's ideas. He bequeathed his entire collection to the prestigious Glenbow Museum in Calgary, and the paintings went into the museum's permanent collection upon his untimely death a few years ago.

The ten paintings in John Davidson's collection tell stories of many aspects of western life, varying in subject matter from lawmen and outlaws to cattle, horses, buffalo, Indians, and mountain men. I am delighted that they have been kept together and am very proud that they are at the Glenbow.

The somber mood of the story dictated the color scheme of the painting. I deliberately put the white sign behind the lawman's head to create a sharp contrast with his beard and the dark underside of his hat. I clearly delineated the prisoner by putting a blank wall behind him. Traditionally, black and white hats distinguished the good guy from the bad guy. The diagonal lines of the plow in the right foreground and the roofline of the barn in the left background lead the viewer's eye to the two riders. The puddle in the foreground adds interest to what would have been a boring foreground element.

The prisoner has a shoulder wound, but he is a lucky man. A peace officer had wide discretion in dealing with rustlers, bandits, and killers. Lawmen such as Wild Bill Hickok and Bat Masterson doled out pistol whippings rather than have a miscreant occupy a cell.

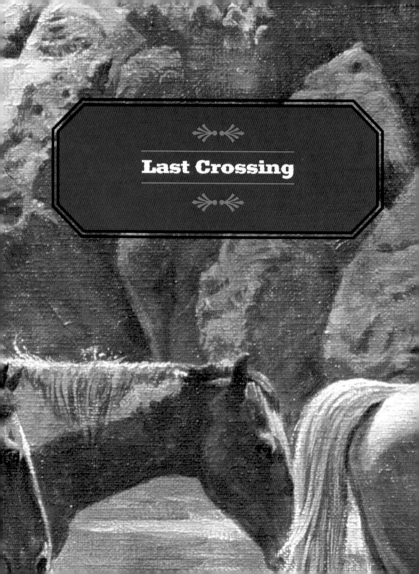

Last Crossing

The setting for this painting is central Arizona, but the action was repeated all over the West: the movement of horses—a most valuable commodity—from one area to another. Moving a herd any distance came with several risks.

Despite its ability to swim, a horse is not necessarily good at crossing rivers; it can drown, drift downstream, or stumble on loose stones in the shallows and break one of its legs. Horses were also subject to snake bites. In the 1870s and '80s, the greatest danger for both the horse herd and its wranglers came from the central band of the Chiricahua Apache led by famed warrior Cochise.

Known as the Southwest's best horsemen, the Apache readily broke wild ponies and used them for work and war when no other mounts were available. The Apache also were the Southwest's best horse thieves. Whether on a raid or on the run, the Apache treated horses as a disposable item, feeding and watering them little and abandoning them when they broke down or became lame.

For a horse-hungry Apache, a stream crossing like the one here was the best time to strike because the wrangler's attention was divided between watching for dangerous serpents sunning on nearby rocks and keeping his animals together and upright. Given the circumstances, the rider in this painting has good reason to be armed and alert.

I had the title, *Last Crossing*, before I started the painting. To emphasize that the horses have traveled for some time, I painted them with their heads low. To add excitement and interest, I gave the cowboy a Winchester, indicating the possibility of danger. To emphasize the cowboy, I placed him against the dark shadows of the rocks and used a rear overhead light to create a sharp light-and-dark contrast between his white hat and the dark rocks.

Lonely Night

The original idea for this painting resulted from my first trip to Arizona in 1968. I was doing research for a painting commissioned by National Geographic.

During some free time, I rode out to Old Tucson, a movie set and tourist attraction. I was surprised by the authenticity of the buildings. Visitors can only see Old Tuscon in the daylight, so I decided to make this a moonlight scene. I was intrigued by the idea of a lone rider coming into town and felt that a cold night would add to the effect of loneliness. One warm color, the light in the window, creates interest and focus. I considered calling this painting *The Stranger*.

The rider in this scene moves down a silent, dark street in Tucson, but he could just as easily be in any of the famous towns in the Old West.

Renegade Brand

Only horse thieves would round

up horses and take them out of a corral at night. The rider in the center of the painting has his Winchester drawn, making it look as though the rustlers have been caught red-handed. Will they fight or run?

To lead the viewer's eye to the center of interest, I deliberately broke the background shape of the mountains with the heads of the horse and rider. The rim of moonlight helps to define the shapes and tell the story.

The horses used as models for this painting were all from Wyoming except for the rearing Appaloosa in the foreground. That

horse was owned by a friend on the north shore of Long Island, not far from where I live. My friend put the stallion through his paces, allowing me to sketch and photograph its many positions and actions. I have since used those sketches and photographs as resource material for many other paintings.

In lonesome West Texas, dry Arizona and New Mexico, and isolated Wyoming, Montana, or the Dakotas, horses were so crucial on the plains that stealing a man's horse essentially condemned him to a slow and painful death. Trials for horse rustling were rare because captured thieves were usually hanged on the spot.

An outbreak of horse rustling in Montana in the early 1880s led moneyed landowner and stockman Granville Stuart to organize some vigilantes known as "Stuart's Stranglers." He drew up a hit list of suspects and sent cowboys to hunt them down and hang them. The Stranglers succeeded, and by 1884 the horse-theft plague that swept the country from Montana to western South Dakota evaporated. If the man in this painting were within Stuart's reach, he would have good reason to pull his rifle.

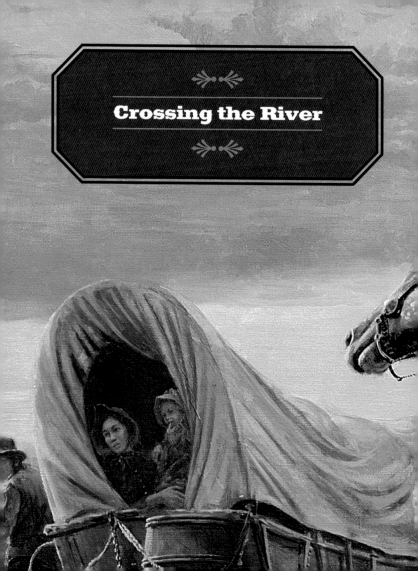

Crossing the River

In this painting, one of four showing a family moving west, I wanted to depict some of the dangers that westward-bound parties encountered. Although the painting is not intended to represent a specific place, these people and wagons could be headed for the Northwest on the Oregon Trail, an overland path to the Pacific Coast used by three hundred thousand pioneers for forty years. Starting at Independence, Missouri, and ending at

Oregon's Columbia River, the trail was busiest from the mid-1840s through the 1850s.

To dramatize the challenges a wagon train faced, I combined the peril of a river crossing with a second, unknown threat from the rear. To create the tension of unseen danger, I have deliberately shown virtually everyone, including the women and children in the wagons, looking in the same direction, to a point out of the picture. The men trying desperately to get the wagons across the river are the only ones not looking back.

The guide in buckskins is silhouetted against the sky with his horse, creating the focus of attention. There is some hope that the cloud of dust in the rear will turn out to be harmless and not from a hostile tribe on the warpath.

What these immigrants packed for the trip, the wagons they chose, and the animals that pulled them were determined by the hard experiences of those who first headed west. A savvy pioneer took a Prairie Schooner or Conestoga wagon, a covered wagon with a slightly curved, water-tight bottom for moving over deeper bodies of water, and high sides that kept equipment and provisions from shifting when negotiating steep grades. These vehicles were often hauled by oxen— hardy, durable animals that Indians did not care to steal. The contents of the wagons were minimal: food, fresh water, clothing, weapons, ammunition, and a few tools. Those who carried heavy equipment— like plows or treasured family furniture—ended up abandoning it when the trail ascended the steep western mountains.

Boundary Line

The theme in this painting is the familiar western story of a land dispute. Fences have been put up, preventing the cattle in the foreground from grazing on the pasture lands and finding water. The ranch house has been turned into an armed camp, and the men at the fence anticipate trouble. Two ranchers in the background have their guns ready in case violence breaks out.

The mountains allowed me to cast shadows over everything except the area behind the two belligerent groups. There I used bright sunlight to create a strong contrast with the dark shapes of the men in the shade. This effect forces the viewer's eye to the center of the painting and the conflict. The vertical composition accents the looming mountains and emphasizes the potential violence. More than one deadly feud in the West started with a scene like this one.

In Montana, Colorado, Wyoming, Nebraska Territory, and other parts of the West, cattlemen let their herds range on government land. Through gentlemen's agreements, different ranchers kept their animals separate by confining their operations to one section or another. The range was public land, and when homesteaders, backed by the federal Homestead Acts, legally staked out portions of the range and fenced it off, they often blocked the way to pastures and water that had been open to all cattlemen for decades.

Barbed wire, developed in the early 1870s, was the most efficient method of fencing and became a symbol of the animosity between homesteaders and cattlemen. By 1879 barbed wire blocked access to enough public land that Montana ranchers started a campaign to assert their grazing rights. Privately, the ranchers and the owners of large cattle companies in other states fought back by cutting the wire and shooting any sodbuster who tried to string up more.

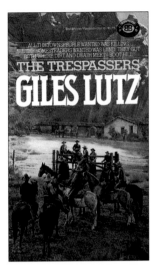

THE TRESPASSERS
GILES LUTZ

Ambush at Scorpion Valley

This 1972 painting was one of the first paperback covers I painted in which I was given complete freedom. I could paint anything I wanted, without any consideration for layout or type

placement. Barbara Bertoli, art director of Avon Books at the time, told me, "Mort, you know more about westerns than I do. Just paint a picture, and we will put it on the cover." Hammer Galleries in New York City later sold this painting the first week it was displayed.

For this book, *Ambush at Scorpion Valley,* by William Colt MacDonald, I was after an eye-catching, action-packed painting to go along with the book's exciting plot. I used the rocks and branches in the lower right foreground to lead the viewer's eye into the action. By putting that element in shadow, I created a dark, simplified shape that leads to the cowboy and horse. The lines of the land in the background all converge on the horse and rider to emphasize them as the center of interest.

Dangerous Crossing

In 1981 I took a trip to Wyoming and stayed at the A-Bar-A Ranch near Encampment. It was a dude ranch that also raised beef cattle. I rode all over the mountains and countryside looking for interesting subjects and scenery to use in paintings.

One day, riding across the North Platte River with the foreman, I realized how carefully the horses crossed. The bottom was very rocky, much like the shoreline in this painting, making the river crossing extremely dangerous for the horses if not done carefully. After climbing onto the shore, I watched the cowboy and horse behind me and immediately came up with the idea of *Dangerous Crossing.*

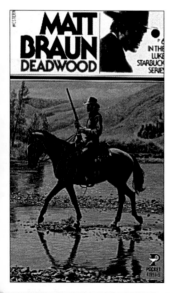

The Winchester in the rider's hand indicates that there is danger from more than the river. The West was a wild place, and cowboys and wranglers constantly had to guard against the threat of thieves, Indians, and snakes.

This painting depicts a place that became famous in the American imagination, the Medicine Bow country of Wyoming. Before the cattlemen ruled here, it was Shoshoni territory. Today it is the Medicine Bow National Forest, protected land where visitors can see the same rich countryside that first lured cowboys in the 1800s.

Holiday Cheer

The basis for a successful narrative

painting is its ability to tell a story quickly. The great American illustrator, artist, and teacher Harvey Dunn said that you should be able to cover the center of interest of a painting with a dollar bill. I think this painting succeeds in that way. The lone cowboy passing the rancher returning from town can be covered with that dollar bill.

By keeping the snow in the background clear of brush or trees, I silhouetted the dark

of the bottle and the figures to create a high contrast area and attract attention. The dark shapes of the mountains on the left and right lead the viewer's eye to the central part of the story.

In the northwest mountains and on the northern plains, winter came early and did not end quickly. The cold season was tough on ranch hands. Time not spent confined to the bunkhouse, the cook house, the stable, or the ranch house involved dashes across a frigid landscape to feed or rescue starving or freezing cows. The forced indoor life was hard on the cowboys psychologically, and working outdoors was tough on everybody physically. The one break the cattle folk had from the rigors and the monotony of winter life was Christmas.

In areas where women were few, the stock men greeted the holiday with childlike enthusiasm. Handmade presents were swapped between the cowhands, and mail-order candy arrived from the East. On small, isolated spreads, Christmas Day might find the hands invited into the ranch owner's home for dinner. An impromptu dance might be held in the barn when there was a fiddler to call the tune, even if the men just danced with each other.

In more populated areas cowboys and ranch hands gathered in small villages or on the largest ranch to hold a serious social, one in which women were present for more traditional dancing. Men marked the occasion by shaving, combing their hair, and wearing their "dress rigs"—fancy western dress distinguished by brocaded or exotic leather vests, a watch chain with a fob, hand-tooled boots, and a large, clean hat.

Sunrise

I came across this rocky outcropping

on a trip to the Arizona desert that inspired several paintings. I was there before sunrise. The lighting effect was so dramatic when the sun started to rise that I felt the scene was perfect for a painting if I could capture it.

I deliberately kept the landscape as the real star of the picture. Putting a lone rider in the painting added interest, but I kept the action to a minimum so that it did not detract from the scene. The cowboy becomes the center of interest as the sunlight catches him and his horse, and his head and hat break the low point of the rock formation.

This scene tells a stark and lonely story. The rider moving into the Arizona sunrise has obviously been up and moving for some time. Although traveling through a desperately hot climate, he is wearing a duster, a linen overcoat to ward off the chill of the desert night. His hat is a wide-brimmed, low-crowned hat meant to keep off the sun when it came up and to sit tight when the hot desert winds rose.

We do not know whether this lone rider is a cowboy, a man headed south to Tombstone to take advantage of a recent silver bonanza, a cowpoke looking for work, or an adventurer seeking his fortune.

After the Rain

A great rock formation and a tree on the A-Bar-A Ranch near Encampment, Wyoming, inspired this painting. During my stay at the ranch, I saw cattle drinking from rain puddles, which gave me the idea for the painting and its title.

To dramatize the rock formation's wonderful shape, I had the sun setting behind it. I always like to have a figure as the center of interest in my paintings. To bring the eye to the lone cowboy, I deliberately put his head above the rocky shape. By having the lightest spot in the painting, the sunlight behind his head, contrast the dark underside of his hat, I directed the viewer's eye to the cowboy.

The greatest danger to the cattle, if they were not grazing in Indian country, was from wild predators such as wolves, bears, cougars, or a coyote pack. Especially in winter, wolves preyed on the herds of Spanish, Mexican, and American cattlemen from the 1600s through the late nineteenth century. At one time, the omnivorous grizzly bear could be found anywhere west of Saint Louis and—especially as cattlemen pushed their herds into places like Colorado, Wyoming, and Montana—the grizzlies often found it much easier to leap on a frightened steer than to run down wild game. Cougars or mountain lions preyed on cattle only when their natural food supplies were depleted. A pack of coyotes could be counted on at anytime and in almost any environment to attack and devour a calf or a weak or injured steer.

Bighorn Rendezvous

In 1983, I met Lou Frederick for the first time at a one-man exhibition of my work at Saks Galleries in Denver. We have been friends ever since. When he invited me on a horseback trek across the Bighorn Mountains, I immediately accepted and two years later we made the trip. Lou, his brother-in-law, Bob, Douglas, and I started on our ride on July 15, 1985, with four horses, one of which carried supplies. The snow was too deep to try any earlier in the year.

On our way to Florence Pass, we came across a monument rock, which would have been perfect for a rendezvous. It was here that I got the idea for this painting. Lou posed as the cowboy looking for an approaching rider. I moved the snow around a bit in the background to focus the viewer's attention on the cowboy, creating great contrast between the dark hat and the white snow.

Later that day when we finally got to Florence Pass, there was a good two feet of snow on the ground, and it had no footprints. We were the first ones through the pass in 1985! The terrain was very rocky, and Bob set out on foot, leading his horse and moving gingerly. Lou went next, on horseback, and I decided if Lou could do it, I could too, and so I stayed mounted, bringing up the rear. Everything was going smoothly until suddenly my horse went down. I have considerable experience with horses, but I had never witnessed a situation like this. As the horse was going down, I remembered reading that cowboys would sometimes encounter a bronco that would deliberately fall and try to roll over on them. The riders would throw themselves clear and then get back on as the horse struggled to get to his feet. I did exactly that and jumped back in the saddle when the horse started to get up. When he was on all fours again, I was still mounted.

Lou and Bob could not believe that an artist from New York City could do what I had done. To this day, we still talk about it!

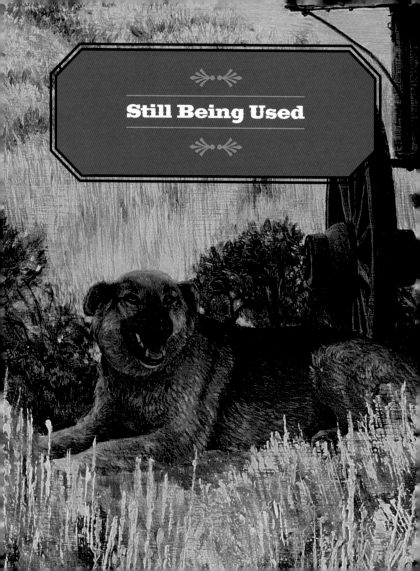

Still Being Used

This old chuck wagon is a landmark
on the A-Bar-A Ranch in Encampment, Wyoming. When I saw it,
I realized it would make a great painting if I could come up with
an idea that would encompass more than a portrait of an abandoned wagon. After considerable thought, I decided to add a dog
taking advantage of the shade from the wagon to escape the heat.

For cowboys the most important element in a trail drive was a cook. If the
cook was bad, he was more reviled than

hostile Indians or hailstorms. If he had any ability, he could become famous among professional cattlemen, but to be an adequate cook he needed a decent chuck wagon.

The chuck wagon carried the bedrolls and personal effects of the cowboys as well as dried foodstuff and ingredients needed for long drives. In addition, it carried paper, pencils, ropes, rifles, ammunition, soap, grease, and kerosene. Strapped on one side was a barrel carrying two days' drinking water. On the other side was a sturdy box carrying shovels, branding irons, farrier equipment, and at least one ax. Bolted to the back was the chuck box with a lid that folded down into a worktable. Inside were pots, pans, utensils, coffee, baking supplies, barber tools, medical supplies, and medicinal whiskey. Driven by the cook, it followed the trail boss or foreman, traveling far ahead of the herd to each day's final destination.

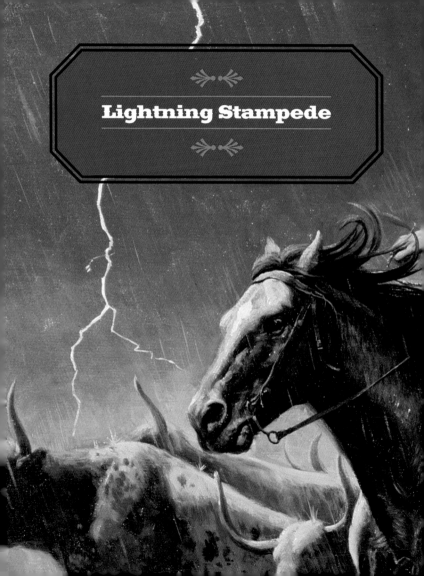

Lightning Stampede

Cowboys on a trail

drive dreaded thunderstorms. A bolt of lightning or a crack of thunder could send a nervous herd dashing across the plains. Animal noises in the night, hail, coyotes, even the banging of a chuck wagon pot could trigger a stampede. To stop an onrushing herd, the cowboys

had to turn the lead cattle into a milling circle—an exceedingly dangerous maneuver. A cowboy would ride up beside the leader to coax it into a turn. If prodding and yelling did not work, he would flail at it with a blanket or fire his pistol near its ears. The dangers to the cowboys intent on stopping the stampede were obvious; they could be gored or trampled. In this painting, I tried to capture the action, excitement, and peril of such a dramatic situation.

Charles Goodnight, a legendary Texas cattleman who pioneered cattle trails, rated stampedes among the worst dangers of the trail. He compared a stampede to an earthquake and noted that excited longhorns gave off incredible body heat during a stampede that was so intense it almost blistered the cowboys.

Riding Point

Riding point was not the safest job on a trail drive, but it was certainly the cleanest. The person leading the herd needed to be an experienced cattle hand who was able to keep a steady, slow pace and not excite the cattle. The man riding point was ahead of the choking clouds of dust that billowed out and backward from the herd. For this reason the "point" did not have to use his neckerchief.

The men riding "drag" ate dust the entire day. The drag riders were the least experienced cowboys and poorest horsemen. The drovers just ahead of them, to the sides of the herd, were "flank" riders. The men ahead of the drovers were the "swing" riders. The "lead" riders showed the most expertise and could anticipate as well as spot trouble. Sometimes, on a very large cattle drive, there were two lead riders. These men often looked to the lead cattle, those who asserted themselves in the herd, to set a pace the other animals could follow.

I emphasized the heat and dust in this painting by utilizing a warm color scheme. The cracked, dry earth in the foreground adds to this effect. In leading the herd, it was important to know what lay ahead as well as what was happening in the rear. I turned the cowboy's head to emphasize the potential danger involved in riding at the head of the herd.

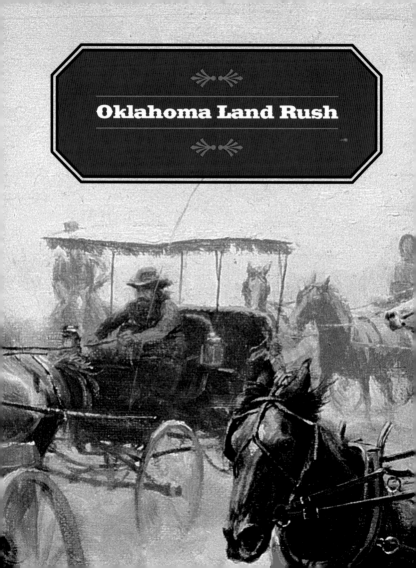

Oklahoma Land Rush

By 1889 incessant pressure to open

the Oklahoma Territory to settlement finally convinced President Benjamin Harrison to authorize a land giveaway. The first Oklahoma Land Rush occurred on April 22, 1889. At the firing of a small cannon, fifty to sixty thousand people raced into the Oklahoma Territory to plant personal stake flags on proposed town lots and quarter-section farm claims.

Those who slipped past army guards before the official opening were dubbed "sooners" and were said to have "jumped the gun."

I had wanted to paint this event for some time, and when I realized 1989 was its hundredth anniversary, I started painting. The subject intrigued me because of the tremendous amount of action, but I was hesitant because of the complexity of the scene. The challenge was to give the effect of thousands of people racing on horseback in an endless sea of dust. I knew I had to show every conceivable kind of rig—buckboards, spring wagons, sulkies, and covered wagons.

I believe I captured the spirit and action of the moment, and I am proud that this painting was the catalog cover for the "Westward Ho!" exhibition of my paintings in 1989 at the Museum of Westward Expansion in Saint Louis. In 1996 the state of Oklahoma installed this painting as a large photo mural in the Oklahoma City welcome centers.

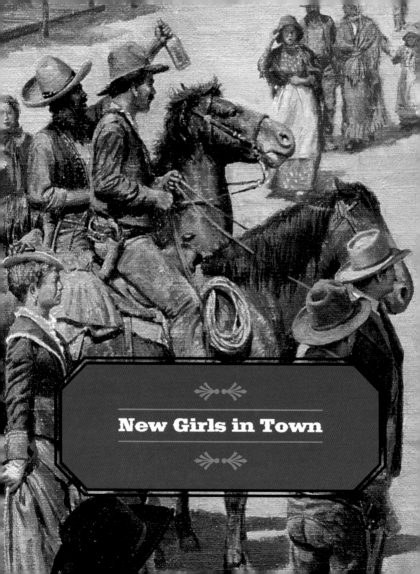

New Girls in Town

The arrival of a stagecoach was always exciting, but these new arrivals would be the subjects of town gossip for weeks to come. Practitioners of the world's oldest profession, they were called "soiled doves" and were a big draw in any town a cowboy visited. Some of the most memorable women in the history of the West are Big Nose Kate, Jenney Silks, and Cattle Kate.

From the appearance of

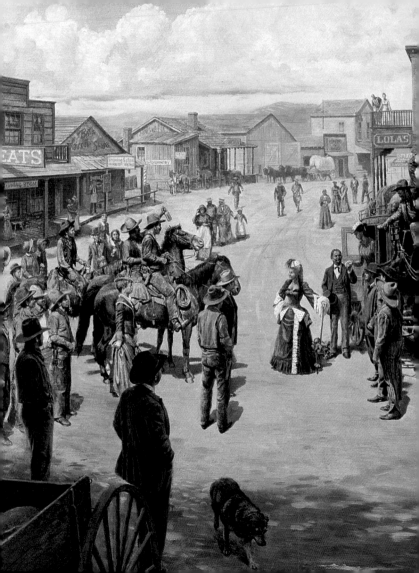

the newest arrival, she probably charged more than the going rate. In a place like Dodge City, time spent upstairs of the Longbranch Saloon with one of its girls cost a dollar. To afford a fancy red dress like the one she wears, a woman needed to be a two-dollar "entertainer."

To call attention to the newly arrived woman, I painted her against the simple background of the street without any figures behind her. She is the only one in the painting silhouetted. Her red dress makes her the brightest spot in the picture. I repeated the red in the sign for Lola's, deliberately associating her with Lola's, the new-comers' ultimate destination.

When a painting has a high viewpoint, it poses a multitude of problems for the artist. Figures in the background must be drawn completely because they are not blocked out by foreground figures. This creates problems of perspective, composition, and drawing that would not arise with a lower eye level. This was one of the most diffi-cult paintings I have ever done. Of course, I get a great deal of satis-faction when a painting of this kind is completed. The fun part was sorting out the reactions of the different townspeople to the arrival of the prostitutes. In general, the women were either angry or curious. The men were happy or curious. The only one bored by it all seems to be the dog in the foreground.

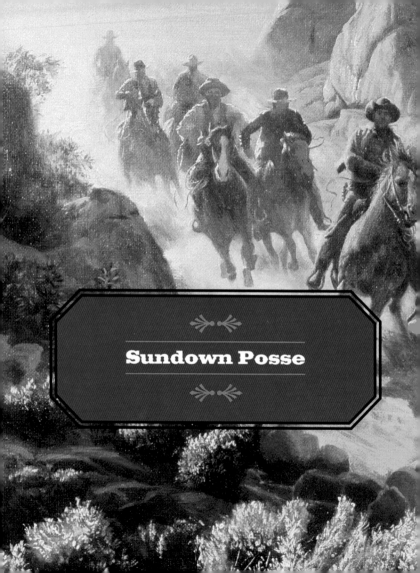

Sundown Posse

During a trip to Arizona in 1982, I took a nighttime Jeep ride into the desert around Phoenix. I witnessed an awesome sunrise, which inspired my painting *Sunrise*. I do not know of a more dramatic lighting effect anywhere. I came across these rocks and immediately envisioned an action scene to contrast the peace and quiet of the desert at that early hour. Back in my studio, I worked with the sketches and photographs I took to create this painting. Because I had just finished *Sunrise,* I changed the time of day and the lighting for this scene to sundown.

This painting of a posse riding into the Arizona dusk could illustrate any story in Arizona's wild history. In 1881, the boomtown of Tombstone was the setting for the legendary clash between the Earps—Wyatt, James, Morgan, and Virgil— and the Clanton and McLaury families. Beginning with the shootout at the O. K. Corral, the feud continued for months.

Arizona and New Mexico were also the setting for the most enduring range war in the West between cattlemen and small ranchers. The most famous episode in this conflict was the 1878 Lincoln County War in New Mexico.

Packing into High Country

I have always found views from heights inspiring, and the scenery in the south central part of Wyoming is tough to beat. While riding around the A-Bar-A Ranch in Encampment, I found this view of the North Platte River to be no exception. What made it even more interesting was that we were not even halfway up the foothills of the Rocky Mountains. This gave me the idea and set the scene for a lone cowboy packing into the high country.

This cowboy and his horses are riding above the North Platte River, which was once the highway of civilization through southern Wyoming. The river is part of the greater Platte river system, a combination of streams said to be one thousand miles long and six inches deep. From this high vantage point the description looks accurate.

The North Platte is one of those rare streams that runs north. Starting in northern Colorado, it runs into Wyoming, near Encampment and to Casper before turning south and east and heading for Nebraska. French explorers followed it in the eighteenth century, and immigrants followed it in the nineteenth. When they reached Wyoming, they ran up against the southern Rocky Mountains, the heights the rider in this painting is slowly climbing. He is on the eastern side of the Continental Divide, the summit of the range.

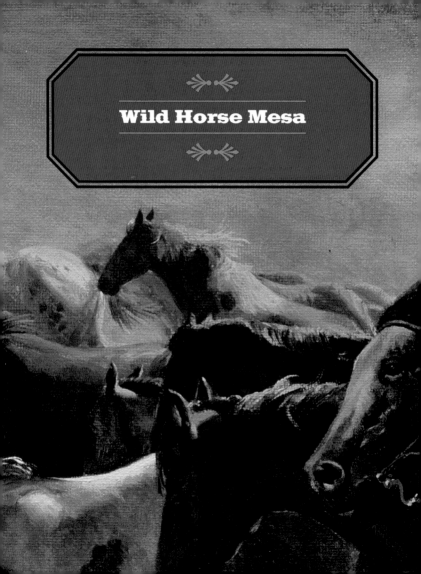

Wild Horse Mesa

This image of a wild horse roundup

is one of the most popular western paintings I have ever done. It was originally reproduced on a Zane Grey paperback called *Wild Horse Mesa,* and so I used the title for the painting. It has subsequently been used as a limited-edition print, a cover for one of my western calendars, a cover for a book of my western paintings, and the cover for this book.

I was after action and excitement, and I found the many and varied motions of the horses in profile provided what I was looking for. I painted the horses kicking up dust to create a horizontal band of light and achieve a strong contrast for the horses and the cowboy. I purposely gave the cowboy a dark beard to highlight him against the light-colored dust and make him a central focus.

The mustangs of Texas and other wild horses in the West came from strays and animals abandoned as lame. Significant wild horse populations roamed Texas and followed the Snake and Columbia Rivers in California. Following the great migration of settlers across the country during the mid-nineteenth century, wild horses became more plentiful on the northern plains, the Rocky Mountains, and especially in Nevada. At their peak, two million horses roamed between the Rio Grande and the Arkansas River while another million were scattered over the rest of the West.

Early Crossing

A trail herd traveled about fifteen

miles a day, and a drive could last as long as two months, depending on the distance from ranch to shipping depot. Among the main hazards along the way were river crossings. Cattle approaching a river were usually thirsty and tended to bunch up along the banks. Cowboys risked their lives driving a herd into and across a river.

The rivers in the path of the herd were generally wild, and many had hazardous banks where cattle and cattlemen could stumble into quicksand or lose their footing on a pebbly bank. Once in the water, cattle would swim, following the lead steers. If those animals became disoriented, the herd could drift far downstream and tired cattle could drown. Consequently, river crossings required a cowboy to get off his horse to help the cattle out of a predicament.

In 1978 I was working on this painting when I met John Davidson for the first time. He had come to my studio to talk to me about a commission. When he saw the unfinished work, he liked it so much he bought it without waiting to see the finished product. I am proud to say it is now in the permanent collection of the Glenbow Museum in Calgary, where he bequeathed it. It has been reproduced in a number of books of my work and has been made into a limited-edition print. In 1982 it was used on the cover of Zane Grey's *Thirty Thousand on the Hoof*. It is one of the most popular western paintings I have done.

Acknowledgments

With special thanks to:

Larry Stone, Ed Curtis, and Peaches Scribner of Rutledge Hill Press for suggesting the idea of publishing twin volumes on cowboys and Indians. As usual, it has been a pleasure to work with them and I am grateful for their encouragement and understanding.

Richard Lynch of Hammer Galleries in New York City, for giving me my first one-man show in 1977 and for bringing my paintings to the attention of the art world.

Howard Shaw and the rest of the staff at Hammer Galleries.

Jane Künstler Broffman and Paula McEvoy, for their invaluable help, not only with this book but in the everyday tasks of managing a busy studio.

My dear Deborah, the wind beneath my wings.

This painting was one of a series I did of a family moving west. It truly became a family affair: I posed for the man while my wife, Deborah, posed for the woman and my grandson Tommy posed for the little boy.

The most difficult thing to achieve in *Prairie Kitchen* was the correct lighting effect. Night and firelight are always tricky to paint. Trying to

capture both, I decided to use the fire as the main source of light and let the shadows go to a dark blue-black.

The first Homestead Act was passed in 1862 and was revised several times over the following decades. It gave public land in the West to settlers like these, who were called sodbusters. The settlers were required to live on the land for five years, build a home, and improve the property. If the sodbuster wanted to own the land before the five years were up, he could buy it for $1.25 per acre. If things did not work out on the homestead within five years, the farmer could pack his wagons and move on with no commitment or obligation.

In the thirty years following the Civil War, some farmers settled on homestead after homestead, moving from the Kansas and Nebraska plains to the Dakotas, Wyoming, and Montana, hoping for good luck and looking for the perfect spread.

Here the wagon train has put in a long day trying to take advantage of good weather. The cowboys' clothing indicates that it is still summer. Some farm wives, like this one, spent a great deal of time sharpening their outdoor-cooking skills. Making camp was hard work, and everyone had a job to do except the little boy playing with a toy locomotive by the campfire. His turn would come soon enough.

The Race

I still remember a scene I saw in a western when I was a kid. The new iron horse and a stagecoach were racing to reach a crossing. I do not recall the name of the movie or how the race turned out, but that memory inspired this painting.

These horses are running hard out, spurred on by the shouts and whip of the driver and the pistol shots of the man riding shotgun. The engineer and train passengers cheer and smile knowing that the old-timers' efforts are futile—they cannot win the race or hold back the wheels of progress.

For much of the nineteenth century, stage service was the most dependable form of transportation in the Old West. Most American cities and towns were linked by coach soon after the Revolutionary War. In the 1840s small stage lines joined frontier communities to the East. In 1850 overland mail service to the West Coast was established, and competition for federal mail carrier contracts provided the impetus for several new stage and freight lines.

The success of the railroad ended the era of stage lines. Businessmen loved the railroad's ability to ship goods quickly, and the government liked the locomotive's capacity as a mail carrier. As early as the 1840s track was being laid all over the West.

When the Central Pacific Railroad met the Union Pacific Railroad at Promontory Point, Utah, in 1869, the country was at last linked by rail, and travel to the West became faster and safer.

In the early 1870s rail and stage passengers occasionally came across one another in scenes like the one shown here. Stage line business quickly dropped away and served only isolated communities, forts, and mining camps and disappeared by the turn of the twentieth century.

Home, Home on the Range

The inspiration for this painting was the title of one of the most famous cowboy tunes of all time. "Home on the Range" was written around 1873 by two Kansans, Daniel E. Kelley and Dr. Brewster Higley, and published in the Kirwin, Kansas, newspaper, the *Chief* on March 21, 1874.

The dust in the distance shows the herd settling down for the night with night riders on watch. Finished with their duties, the other cowboys have camped a safe distance from the herd to prevent spooking the cattle with the clatter of pots and pans.

As soon as dusk fell on a trail drive, cowboys like these ate and grabbed a nap. Each man had to stand two hours of night watch over the herd, and those who had the second shift were given only a couple hours' sleep before their watch. While these men slept, the rest wound down from their day. Some of the men have already eaten. The cook pours coffee while some hands go for an extra portion of chow.

During the long, hot days on the drive, the cowboys looked forward to sitting around the campfire each night. In this painting the glow of the fire bathes the men in warm light, which contrasts with the cool blues of the evening sky. A guitar and accordion have appeared, and several of the men join in singing. Relaxed, the cowboys smoked, chatted, and sang their favorite trail tunes. Singing was not only entertaining but useful as well. On night watch, cowboys sang to the cattle to keep them quiet and calm. Campfire singing allowed the hands to swap songs and expand their repertoires.

Each cowboy knows that tomorrow will bring hard work and unknown dangers, but tonight they enjoy the tranquillity of the camp, their home on the range.

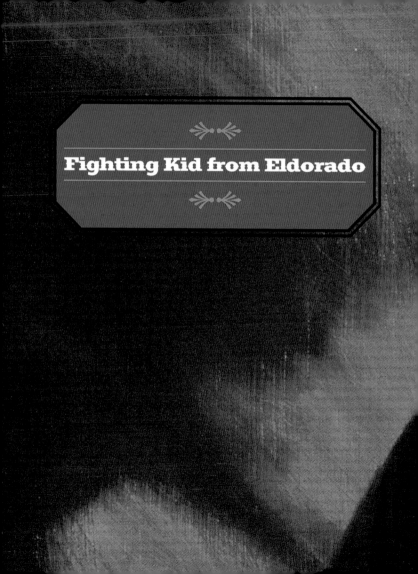

Fighting Kid from Eldorado

I think everyone knows the ritual of

a showdown between an outlaw and a lawman, facing each other on a dusty street, their hands ready to draw their guns. We have seen it depicted in movies and television dramas and read about it in western novels. In the legendary conflict between gunfighters and lawmen, more often than not, the lawman had been a gunfighter and the outlaw a former lawman. The line between them could be rather fine.

Being mean or fast was not always the trait that got a gunslinging lawman through the fight. Wild Bill Hickok's first recorded gunfight took place in 1861, when he was twenty-four. He killed three men in

a quarrel. After scouting for the Union army in the Civil War and then for the cavalry, he became a peace officer in Kansas in the early 1870s, serving in Hays City and famously in Abilene. He was successful in gunfights because he never panicked.

This painting was one of a series of paperback book covers I did in the 1960s featuring various gunfighters and lawmen in action. I chose a stormy red sky for drama and had the sky toward the horizon go light to create a contrast with the dark butt of the gun, emphasizing the action of the gunfighter about to draw his weapon.

The Free Lands